THE U.S. GOVERNMENT
HOW IT WORKS

THE
PRESIDENCY

THE U.S. GOVERNMENT
HOW IT WORKS

★ ★ ★

THE CENTRAL INTELLIGENCE AGENCY
THE DEPARTMENT OF HOMELAND SECURITY
THE FEDERAL BUREAU OF INVESTIGATION
THE HOUSE OF REPRESENTATIVES
THE PRESIDENCY
THE SENATE
THE SUPREME COURT

THE U.S. GOVERNMENT
HOW IT WORKS

THE
PRESIDENCY

HEATHER LEHR WAGNER

CHELSEA HOUSE
PUBLISHERS
An imprint of Infobase Publishing

The Presidency

Chelsea House
An imprint of Infobase Publishing
132 West 31st Street
New York, NY 10001

ISBN-10: 0-7910-9284-4
ISBN-13: 978-0-7910-9284-2

Library of Congress Cataloging-in-Publication Data
Wagner, Heather Lehr.
  The presidency / Heather Lehr Wagner.
    p. cm.—(The U.S. government: how it works)
  Includes bibliographical references and index.
  ISBN 0-7910-9284-4 (hardcover)
  1. Presidents—United States—Juvenile literature.   I. Title.   II. Series.

  JK517.W34 2007
  352.230973—dc22

                                        2006028513

Chelsea House books are available at special discounts when purchased in bulk quantities for businesses, associations, institutions, or sales promotions. Please call our Special Sales Department in New York at (212) 967–8800 or (800) 322–8755.

You can find Chelsea House on the World Wide Web at
http://www.chelseahouse.com

Series design by James Scotto-Lavino
Cover design by Ben Peterson

Printed in the United States of America

Bang NMSG 10 9 8 7 6 5 4 3 2 1

This book is printed on acid-free paper.

All links and Web addresses were checked and verified to be correct at the time of publication. Because of the dynamic nature of the Web, some addresses and links may have changed since publication and may no longer be valid.

CONTENTS

1

INAUGURATION

Every American president begins his term in office with the same sentence: "I do solemnly swear (or affirm) that I will faithfully execute the office of President of the United States, and will to the best of my ability, preserve, protect, and defend the Constitution of the United States."

Since April 30, 1789, when George Washington stepped onto the balcony of Federal Hall in New York City, 42 men have begun their terms as president with the same phrase. But all of these men have put their own stamp on the office of president of the United States, and the executive branch has evolved as a reflection of their personalities and their visions for the country.

Today, when we think about our national government, the president is often the clearest and most visible symbol of that government at work. But when the Founding

7

This 1889 painting by Ramon de Elorriaga, *The Inauguration of George Washington,* depicts his swearing-in on April 30, 1789, at Federal Hall in New York City.

Fathers first met in Philadelphia in 1787 to discuss how to shape the new government that would become the United States, the scope of the presidency sparked intense debate. Some questioned the need for a single individual to lead the government, fearing that a strong head of government would quickly lead to a monarchy. It soon became clear, however, that the leader of the new government must have enough power to be independent of the legislature and enough power to ensure that the federal government would not be at the mercy of the state governments.

Other debates centered on how the new executive would be elected—by popular vote, by designated electors, or by Congress—and how long his term in office would last. Another debate focused on whether the chief executive should have a specified council of advisors, perhaps from specific branches of the government, such as the president of the Senate and the chief justice of the Supreme Court, or from specific areas of the country, like a representative from the East, the Middle States, and the South.

When it became clear that George Washington, hero of the Revolutionary War, would be the first nominee for president of the United States, many of the debates were resolved. The idea of a council of advisors was set aside; the Constitution does not even call for a "cabinet." The president was given the right of veto power over legislation. He was given the right to appoint people to office "in all not otherwise provided for." He was given the title of "commander in chief."

The final results of the debates and discussions outlined the terms, seen in Article II of the U.S. Constitution, that govern the presidency—terms that have, with only a few additional amendments, dictated the scope of the office for more than 200 years. The Constitution notes that the president shall hold office for a term of four years. It states how the president shall be elected and removed from office.

The Constitution specifies that the president must be a natural-born citizen of the United States (a citizen who was born in this country). It specifies that the president must be at least 35 years old and have lived within the United States for at least 14 years.

The Constitution notes that the president should be paid for the service performed and that the salary should neither increase nor decrease during the president's term in office. It notes the oath of office that must be spoken for each new president.

The Constitution also states that the president has the power to grant reprieves and pardons, to make treaties, and to appoint ambassadors and judges of the Supreme Court. Finally, the Constitution states that the president should periodically give Congress information on the state of the union, and be responsible for executing the laws of the United States faithfully.

These broad but simple guidelines provided an outline of the office of the president for the first man to hold that title. It was up to future presidents to fill in the details that would make the office of president one of the most powerful in the world.

THE FIRST PRESIDENT

Just as the drafters of the Constitution had George Washington in mind when considering the position of president, Washington himself, as the first holder of the office, placed an imprint on the presidency that would last more than two centuries. Washington understood that he was setting a precedent that future presidents would follow, and it is to his credit that so many of the standards he set would prove valuable guidelines for the nation's leadership.

Washington created a strong cabinet of four men, including Thomas Jefferson as secretary of state and Alexander Hamilton as secretary of the treasury. All loans and debts that the country undertook were subject to Washington's approval. Washington required his approval for any use of the seal of the United States. He successfully used his popularity to build a strong relationship with Congress, and he was careful to treat members of the Senate and the House of Representatives with respect. He felt strongly that the presidency must be dignified, using symbols and ceremony when necessary. He set the precedent of serving only two terms as president, and all future presidents (with one exception—Franklin D. Roosevelt, who was elected to four terms in office) would follow this example. In fact, Washington had wanted to serve only one term but reluctantly agreed to serve an additional four years. Washington was so popular that it seems certain he could have been elected president for life, had he chosen. The Twenty-second Amendment to the Constitution (ratified in 1951) limited future presidents to two terms.

Washington set an example that other presidents would follow of traveling around the country, so that people throughout the United States could have an opportunity to see their leader and so that he could be familiar with various states and their differing needs. Washington assumed that the president would be actively involved in shaping foreign and domestic policy, and his assertive attitude toward both ensured that future presidents would clearly be at the head of government policymaking.

IN THE BEGINNING

Just as every presidency begins with the same oath of office, so every presidency begins with a ceremony known as the inauguration. The inauguration marks the transition from one president to the next; it is the official beginning of a new administration. With the recitation of the oath of office, a private citizen formally becomes president. The results of a presidential election are decided weeks earlier, with the tallying of electoral votes, but it is the inauguration that formally marks the time when a president begins his term in office.

Again, this precedent was set by George Washington, who traveled from his home in Mount Vernon, Virginia, to the nation's capital (then located in New York City) after being informed of his election on April 14, 1789. Ceremonies, parades, and the noise of ringing bells and booming cannons accompanied him on his trip north. Parties and

WASHINGTON'S RECEPTION BY THE LADIES, ON PASSING THE
BRIDGE AT TRENTON, N. J. APRILL 1789,
ON HIS WAY TO NEW YORK TO BE INAUGURATED FIRST PRESIDENT OF THE UNITED STATES.

An 1845 lithograph by Nathaniel Currier shows George
Washington being greeted by a group of women in
Trenton, New Jersey, as he travels to his inauguration in
New York City. Ceremonies and parades followed Wash-
ington as he made his way from his home in Virginia to
New York.

celebrations in New York delayed the official inauguration for several days. During the time before the inauguration, one final debate raged: Exactly what would the leader of the new nation be called? Among the proposals was "His Highness the President of the United States of America and Protector of Their Liberties." In the end, it was decided that the chief executive would be simply known as "The President of the United States."

The first inauguration drew large crowds to New York. Washington began the tradition of delivering an inaugural address (or speech) at the ceremony. In his first address, Washington expressed his conflicted feelings about accepting the call to serve as president. Washington also noted his decision to refuse any payment for his service as president. This was one of the few acts Washington took that did not become a precedent for future presidents.

Many notable events have marked presidential inaugurations over the years. Washington began the custom of taking the oath of office outdoors, and he used the phrase "So help me God" after the oath. There was an inaugural ball after Washington's inauguration, but because of other business it was not held until May 7. First Lady Martha Washington did not travel to New York for her husband's inauguration.

In his second inauguration, on March 4, 1793, Washington set a record, of sorts. He delivered the shortest inaugural address—a mere 135 words.

John Adams, the second president, began the custom of receiving the oath from the chief justice of the

WASHINGTON'S SECOND INAUGURAL ADDRESS

On March 4, 1793, George Washington delivered his second inaugural address in the city that was then serving as the nation's capital—Philadelphia. Like so many of Washington's acts, this one was noteworthy—as the shortest inaugural speech given by any president.

Fellow Citizens:

I am again called upon by the voice of my country to execute the functions of its Chief Magistrate. When the occasion proper for it shall arrive, I shall endeavor to express the high sense I entertain of this distinguished honor, and of the confidence which has been reposed in me by the people of united America.

Previous to the execution of any official act of the President the Constitution requires an oath of office. This oath I am now about to take, and in your presence: That if it shall be found during my administration of the Government I have in any instance violated willingly or knowingly the injunctions thereof, I may (besides incurring constitutional punishment) be subject to the upbraidings of all who are now witnesses of the present solemn ceremony.

Supreme Court. Thomas Jefferson, the third president, was the first to take the oath of office in the new capital, Washington, D.C.

Martin Van Buren (1837) started the custom of having the outgoing (Andrew Jackson) and incoming presidents ride together to the Capitol for the inauguration. African Americans first participated in the inaugural parade in 1865, when Abraham Lincoln began his second term in office. Women did not participate in an inaugural parade until 1917, when Woodrow Wilson began his second term as president.

The Twentieth Amendment to the Constitution changed the inaugural date to January 20, specifying that the president's term would end at noon on that date. Franklin D. Roosevelt was the first president to be inaugurated on this date, beginning his second term as president on January 20, 1937.

The first inauguration to be televised was in 1949, when Harry Truman began his second term in office. And it was Bill Clinton's second inauguration, in 1997, that marked the first live broadcast of the ceremony on the Internet.

INAUGURATIONS TODAY

Inaugurations for modern presidents follow many of the precedents set long ago. Presidents-elect have attended a morning worship service before the inaugural ceremony since 1933. The outgoing president then accompanies the president-elect to the swearing-in ceremony at the Capitol.

The chief justice of the Supreme Court administers the oath of office. After the swearing-in, the new president delivers an inaugural address, which generally outlines his plans for his term in office. George Washington's second inaugural address was the shortest; the longest, delivered by William Henry Harrison in 1841, was 8,445 words—so long that Harrison began the address, stopped to take the oath of office, and then resumed the speech. Harrison died one month later of pneumonia, believed to have been caused by prolonged exposure to bitterly cold weather on his Inaugural Day.

Some presidents have used the inaugural address to deliver inspiring messages to the nation that have lasted long after their terms ended. In 1865, as the Civil War was drawing to an end, Abraham Lincoln encouraged the nation: "With malice toward none, with charity for all, with firmness in the right as God gives us to see the right, let us strive on to finish the work we are in, to bind up the nation's wounds, to care for him who shall have borne the battle and for his widow and his orphan, to do all which may achieve and cherish a just and lasting peace among ourselves and with all nations." In 1933, as the Great Depression swept over the United States, Franklin D. Roosevelt's inaugural address contained the bracing message: "The only thing we have to fear is fear itself." And in 1961, John F. Kennedy encouraged a new generation to "ask not what your country can do for you—ask what you can do for your country."

After the inaugural ceremony, the new president, vice president, and guests enjoy a luncheon at the U.S. Capitol. The president views an inaugural parade from a viewing stand, and later a series of inaugural balls are held in the president's honor. The number has varied over the

Four presidents—past, present, and future—attended the inauguration of John F. Kennedy in January 1961. Here, Kennedy shakes hands with his predecessor, Dwight Eisenhower. To the right is Lyndon Johnson, Kennedy's vice president, who would become president in 1963 after Kennedy's assassination. At far right is Richard Nixon, who was vice president under Eisenhower; he would be elected president in 1968.

years—in 1997, 14 balls marked President Bill Clinton's inauguration.

For more than two centuries, a president's term in office has begun in the same way—with an inauguration—and

with the same oath of office. But within that simple vow
to "preserve, protect, and defend the Constitution of the
United States," an extraordinary range of power and responsibility is placed on each new president. What exactly
does it mean to be the president of the United States? How
does the president shape policy? How has the president's
role changed over the years? In the chapters that follow,
we will discover the answers to these questions and learn
what it is like to be the president of the United States.

2

THE PRESIDENT AND THE CONSTITUTION

The rules that shape the presidency, stating who can be president, what the president's powers will be, and how long he or she will serve, are found in the Constitution. In several paragraphs, the presidency is defined.

These paragraphs, though, were among the most difficult to resolve when the men charged with creating the Constitution met in Philadelphia in 1787. The debates over the presidency were among the bitterest disagreements at the Constitutional Convention.

The 55 delegates to the convention represented 12 of the 13 original states (Rhode Island did not send delegates).

George Washington is shown in this 1856 painting by Junius Brutus Stearns, *George Washington Addressing the Constitutional Convention.* One issue debated at the Constitutional Convention in 1787 was whether the executive branch would consist of several men acting as a council or would be led by a single individual. Other issues involved veto powers and the term of office.

They were, for the most part, in agreement over the need to shape a new system of government. They largely agreed that the government should be divided into separate branches—the executive, judicial, and legislative branches—to ensure a balance of power. But the question of what the executive branch would involve exposed the fears and misgivings of the delegates.

The initial proposal was that the executive branch would consist of several men, forming a kind of committee or council. The issues that had led to the Revolutionary War were still fresh in the minds of the delegates, and many feared duplicating the same form of government— a monarchy ruled by a king—that they had so recently fought against.

James Wilson from Pennsylvania was the one who first proposed the idea of an executive branch headed by a single individual. A long silence followed his suggestion, finally broken by Edmund Randolph of Virginia, who reminded Wilson that a single executive might be the beginning of a monarchy in the United States.

Another proposal, from Roger Sherman of Connecticut, focused on how the members of the executive branch would be chosen. Sherman felt that the executive branch's responsibility should be to carry out the will of the American people, as expressed by the legislative branch. In Sherman's proposal, the executive branch would report to the legislative branch, and the legislative branch would decide what business the executive branch should handle and how many executives should be appointed at any one time to handle this business.

Some—but not all—of the objections became more muted as it became clear that George Washington, who was serving as the president of the Constitutional Convention, might become the first "chief executive." The scope of the powers of this "president," as the chief executive became known, also drew concern. Some feared the idea of a president powerful enough to serve as commander-in-chief and also make treaties and appoint government

Roger Sherman, a delegate to the Constitutional Convention from Connecticut, thought that the executive branch should report to the legislative branch. He also was opposed to the idea of allowing the person leading the executive branch to be re-elected.

officials. Others worried about how the president would be chosen, fearing that few men would be popular enough to win a clear majority of the votes. Still others worried about what would happen if the president proved unwilling to give up his office, warning of the dangers of a president "for life."

This question of how long a president should serve was a critical one for many of the delegates. Wilson, the delegate who initially proposed a single executive, or president, favored a three-year term, with the idea that after this short period a president might be eligible for re-election. Sherman and others opposed the idea of re-election, believing that a single term provided the best protection for the country against a president who might prove unworthy once in office. Still others favored a single term of seven years, or a fixed number of terms after which a president could no longer be elected.

It took four months for the delegates to resolve their disagreements and emerge from Philadelphia with a Constitution for the United States. The debates did not end with the final Constitution, however. Many continued to question the need for a president and expressed their concerns about limiting his powers. The questions about who should be president, and how much power should be connected to the office, continue to this day.

THE ROUGH DRAFT

The earliest draft of the document that would eventually become the Constitution was known as "the Virginia Plan" and was presented to the Constitutional Convention by the governor of Virginia, Edmund Randolph. Most experts agree that its author was probably James Madison.

The Virginia Plan called for a "National Executive," to be chosen by the "National Legislature" (or Congress). The number of years this executive would serve was left blank, but a note was included that said the executive could not serve more than one term.

It is interesting to look at the Virginia Plan and the earliest debates at the convention to see how the United States might have become quite a different nation had the delegates not revised their plans for the presidency. The initial agreement among the delegates was that the president would serve one term of seven years and that he could not be re-elected after these seven years.

The proposal to have the executive chosen by Congress proved unworkable. It destroyed the idea of balance of power by giving too much power to the legislative branch. The delegates decided to combine the proposals of a president chosen by popular vote and by representatives of the people with an "Electoral College." States would be divided into a certain number of districts (in the rough draft this number was left blank), and voters would elect a certain number of representatives (again, the number was left blank), who would meet and elect by ballot the person who would become the chief executive. It was noted that the Electoral College could not select one of its own members to serve as chief executive.

Later discussions determined that the state legislatures should choose the "electors" who would make up the Electoral College. The question of how long the president should serve again arose. Another proposal at this early stage was that the president should serve for six years and be eligible for re-election but also that he could be impeached and removed from office if he should prove incompetent.

The Virginia Plan also called for the executive branch to have a "veto power" (a power to reject acts of the legislature), and this was also hammered out in the debates. Benjamin Franklin argued against the chief executive being able to veto acts of Congress, having seen this power abused by the governor of his state of Pennsylvania.

Next, the delegates debated the question of what power the president should have to appoint other officials. The delegates decided that the president could have the power to pick federal judges but that the Senate would have the power to reject his nominees if a majority of its members agreed.

The first draft of the Constitution described a president (the first draft used the term "president" instead of "chief executive" or "executive") appointed by the Congress who would serve a single seven-year term. The president would have the power to veto acts of Congress, would command the armed forces, and could be impeached and removed from office.

CONTINUING DEBATES

Once this rough draft was circulated, the debates about the presidency began again. The delegates agreed that the president must meet certain standards—he must be a certain age, must have been a citizen of the United

States for a specific period of time. There was disagreement, though, about what other qualifications the president should have.

One delegate—Charles Pinckney of South Carolina—felt that the men selected to serve in the executive, legislative, and judicial branches of the government should all be required to own a certain amount of property, suggesting that wealth would keep them independent. Pinckney's idea was that the president's personal wealth should be at least $100,000, a considerable sum in those days. This point was hotly debated by several delegates, including Benjamin Franklin, who argued that the United States should not demonstrate such clear favoritism for the wealthy.

Other debates focused on whether the Congress or the president should have war powers. It was decided that the president should have the ability to respond in the event of a sudden attack, although the Constitution gives Congress the power to declare war.

There was discussion about whether a council of advisors to the president, or a "cabinet," should be included in the Constitution. Debate focused on who these men might be—one proposal was for the cabinet to consist of the president of the Senate, the chief justice of the Supreme Court, and the ministers of foreign and domestic affairs, war, and finance.

There was also debate about who should replace the president if he died, resigned, or was forced from office. Proposals stated that the duties of the president would be

FRANKLIN IN THE NATIONAL CONVENTION.

Benjamin Franklin addresses the Constitutional Convention in this engraving. Franklin spoke against a proposal by Charles Pinckney of South Carolina that would have required the president to have a personal wealth of at least $100,000, a princely sum in those days. Franklin did not want such favoritism to be shown to the wealthy.

performed by the president of the Senate, the chief justice, the members of the cabinet, or a suitable candidate chosen by Congress should the need arise.

With all of the competing proposals and debates, it is astonishing that the majority of the delegates finally signed the polished and revised Constitution on September 17, 1787. The required nine states ratified the document by June 21, 1788. The questions of who would serve as president, for how long, and what powers he would have, were resolved—as least for a while.

IN THE CONSTITUTION

Several portions of the Constitution deal with the presidency. It is interesting to compare what was discussed in the debates with what became the final text of the Constitution:

Article I. Section 7

. . . Every bill which shall have passed the House of Representatives and the Senate shall, before it become a law, be presented to the President of the United States; if he approve he shall sign it, but if not he shall return it, with his objections to that House in which it shall have originated, who shall enter the objections at large on their Journal, and proceed to reconsider it. If after such reconsideration two thirds of that House shall agree to pass the bill, it shall be sent, together with the objections, to the other House, by which it shall likewise be reconsidered, and if approved by two thirds of that House, it shall become a law. . . .

Article II. Section 1

The executive power shall be vested in a President of the United States of America. He shall hold his office during the term of four years, and, together with the Vice President, chosen for the same term, be elected, as follows.

Each state shall appoint, in such manner as the Legislature thereof may direct, a number of electors, equal to the whole number of senators and representatives to which the state may be entitled in the Congress: but no senator or representative, or person holding an office of trust or profit under the United States, shall be appointed an elector. . . .

No person except a natural born citizen, or a citizen of the United States, at the time of the adoption of this Constitution, shall be eligible to the office of president; neither shall any person be eligible to that office who shall not have attained to the age of thirty five years, and been fourteen years a resident within the United States.

In case of the removal of the President from office, or of his death, resignation, or inability to discharge the powers and duties of the said office, the same shall devolve on the Vice President, and the Congress may by law provide for the case of removal, death, resignation or inability, both of the President and Vice President, declaring what officer shall then act as President, and such officer shall act accordingly, until the disability be removed, or a President shall be elected.

The President shall, at stated times, receive for his services, a compensation, which shall neither be increased nor diminished during the period for which he shall have been elected. . . .

Before he enter on the execution of his office, he shall take the following oath or affirmation:—"I do solemnly swear (or affirm) that I will faithfully execute the office of President of the United States, and will to the best of my ability, preserve, protect and defend the Constitution of the United States."

Section 2

The President shall be Commander in Chief of the Army and Navy of the United States, and of the militia of the several states. . . .

He shall have power, by and with the advice and consent of the Senate, to make treaties, provided two thirds of the senators present concur; and he shall nominate, and by and with the advice and consent of the Senate, shall appoint ambassadors, other public ministers and consuls, judges of the Supreme Court, and all other officers of the United States, whose appointments are not herein otherwise provided for. . . .

Section 3

He shall from time to time give to the Congress information of the State of the Union, and recommend to their consideration such measures as he shall judge necessary and expedient. . . . He shall take care that the laws be faithfully executed, and shall commission all the officers of the United States.

U.S. PRESIDENTS AND WHEN THEY SERVED

★ ★ ★ ★ ★

President	Term in Office
1. George Washington	April 30, 1789–March 4, 1797
2. John Adams	March 4, 1797–March 4, 1801
3. Thomas Jefferson	March 4, 1801–March 4, 1809
4. James Madison	March 4, 1809–March 4, 1817
5. James Monroe	March 4, 1817–March 4, 1825
6. John Quincy Adams	March 4, 1825–March 4, 1829
7. Andrew Jackson	March 4, 1829–March 4, 1837
8. Martin Van Buren	March 4, 1837–March 4, 1841
9. William Henry Harrison	March 4, 1841–April 4, 1841
10. John Tyler	April 4, 1841–March 4, 1845
11. James Polk	March 4, 1845–March 4, 1849
12. Zachary Taylor	March 4, 1849–July 9, 1850
13. Millard Fillmore	July 9, 1850–March 4, 1853
14. Franklin Pierce	March 4, 1853–March 4, 1857
15. James Buchanan	March 4, 1857–March 4, 1861
16. Abraham Lincoln	March 4, 1861–April 15, 1865
17. Andrew Johnson	April 15, 1865–March 4, 1869
18. Ulysses Grant	March 4, 1869–March 4, 1877
19. Rutherford Hayes	March 4, 1877–March 4, 1881
20. James Garfield	March 4, 1881–September 19, 1881
21. Chester Arthur	September 19, 1881–March 4, 1885
22. Grover Cleveland	March 4, 1885–March 4, 1889

President	Term in Office
23. Benjamin Harrison	March 4, 1889–March 4, 1893
24. Grover Cleveland	March 4, 1893–March 4, 1897
25. William McKinley	March 4, 1897–September 14, 1901
26. Theodore Roosevelt	September 14, 1901–March 4, 1909
27. William Taft	March 4, 1909–March 4, 1913
28. Woodrow Wilson	March 4, 1913–March 4, 1921
29. Warren Harding	March 4, 1921–August 2, 1923
30. Calvin Coolidge	August 2, 1923–March 4, 1929
31. Herbert Hoover	March 4, 1929–March 4, 1933
32. Franklin Roosevelt	March 4, 1933–April 12, 1945
33. Harry Truman	April 12, 1945–January 20, 1953
34. Dwight Eisenhower	January 20, 1953–January 20, 1961
35. John Kennedy	January 20, 1961–November 22, 1963
36. Lyndon Johnson	November 22, 1963–January 20, 1969
37. Richard Nixon	January 20, 1969–August 9, 1974
38. Gerald Ford	August 9, 1974–January 20, 1977
39. Jimmy Carter	January 20, 1977–January 20, 1981
40. Ronald Reagan	January 20, 1981–January 20, 1989
41. George H.W. Bush	January 20, 1989–January 20, 1993
42. Bill Clinton	January 20, 1993–January 20, 2001
43. George W. Bush	January 20, 2001–

Section 4

The President, Vice President and all civil officers of the United States, shall be removed from office on impeachment for, and conviction of, treason, bribery, or other high crimes and misdemeanors.

AMENDMENTS

The Constitution, particularly Article II, provided the initial definition of the presidency. Later amendments to the Constitution would offer additional clarification to the office.

The Twelfth Amendment, ratified in 1804, added further details about the Electoral College, and how the president and vice president would be elected. Until this time, the presidential candidate receiving the greatest number of votes would become president; the runner-up would become vice president. This created an unworkable situation in which representatives from different political parties, often with vastly different visions for the country, would then be expected to join together cooperatively as president and vice president. In the Twelfth Amendment, candidates would now clearly run for election as either president or vice president.

The beginning of the presidential term was changed from March 4 to January 20 (a new term beginning at noon on that day) in the Twentieth Amendment, ratified in 1933. In 1951, the Twenty-second Amendment specified that the president would be limited to two terms (President Franklin D. Roosevelt had been elected to four terms as president but died before completing his fourth term). The Twenty-fifth Amendment, ratified in 1967, gave the president the power, with approval from Congress, to appoint a vice president when the vice presidency became vacant (President Richard Nixon soon had to follow this amendment, appointing Gerald Ford to the vice presidency in 1973 when Vice President Spiro Agnew was forced to resign). The Twenty-fifth Amendment also specified that the vice president would become president if the president died, resigned, or was removed from office. Once again, this amendment would apply to Gerald Ford, who became president when Richard Nixon resigned in 1974.

Other amendments to the Constitution—those amendments that specify who has the right to vote—also have shaped the presidency. The Fifteenth Amendment, ratified in 1870, gave the right to vote to blacks. Women were given the right to vote in 1920, with the ratification of the Nineteenth Amendment. And eighteen-year-olds gained the right to vote in 1971, with passage of the Twenty-sixth Amendment (previously voters needed to be at least 21 years of age).

3

THE POWERS OF
THE PRESIDENT

The Constitution spelled out several powers reserved for the executive branch. These included the power to serve as commander in chief of the armed forces, the power to make treaties, the power to make political appointments, and the power to veto certain acts of Congress. Throughout history, presidents have chosen to exercise these powers in different ways. Sometimes they tested the limits of the Constitution or proved the wisdom of the Founding Fathers in granting these powers to the presidency.

The Constitution gives the president the power to serve as "Commander in Chief of the Army and Navy of the United States, and of the Militia of the several States." The U.S. military has expanded well beyond the small volunteer forces initially envisioned by the delegates to the Constitutional Convention, and the power to serve as commander in chief places in the president's hands access to a large, well-equipped fighting force and a wide array of weapons systems, including nuclear weapons.

What happens when presidents choose to exercise this power? And how many presidents have the kind of military experience necessary to truly direct the armed forces of the United States?

George Washington's experience as a Revolutionary War hero made him the clear choice to be the country's first president, and his proven skills in battle made it seem apparent that a president could serve as commander in chief. In fact, Washington did actually lead soldiers in the field after becoming president, riding at the head of troops to put down a rebellious force of some 6,000 men who had assembled near Pittsburgh to protest a tax on whiskey. It would be the first and only time a sitting president would lead troops into the field.

As president, James Madison was present at Bladensburg, Maryland, when American forces were defeated by British troops and forced to retreat during the War of 1812. The British then marched to Washington, burning government buildings, including the Capitol and the White House. President Abraham Lincoln traveled to Fort Stevens in Washington, D.C., in July 1864 to survey the scene, when his Union soldiers came under fire from Confederate forces. Lincoln was quickly rushed back to the White House.

In more recent years, presidents have traveled to war zones to meet with U.S. forces, but safety and security concerns make it impossible to imagine contemporary presidents leading troops into conflict. Presidents have sent Americans into combat both close to and far from U.S. soil.

Washington was the first, but certainly not the last, president to be elected based on a successful military career. Andrew Jackson became a military hero after his success at the Battle of New Orleans during the War of 1812. Jackson had also served in the Continental Army during the Revolutionary War and is the only American president to have been held as a prisoner of war. William Henry Harrison also had a distinguished military career during the War of 1812, earning fame for his command of troops during the Battle of the Thames. Zachary Taylor's military achievements during the Mexican-American War made him a national hero and, later, a successful candidate for president. Ulysses Grant earned fame as a commander of Union troops during the Civil War. Theodore Roosevelt's achievements during the Spanish-American War brought him national attention, and Dwight Eisenhower was sought after as a presidential candidate by both the Republican and Democratic parties after his service as Supreme Allied Commander during World War II.

Although military service is not a requirement for the presidency, many of the men who have become president have had some form of military service. Not all, however, have seen active combat. In fact, only a few former presidents have not served in the military, militia, or

Theodore Roosevelt leads the Rough Riders into battle during the Spanish-American War. Several presidents parlayed their success on the battlefield into a run for the nation's highest office.

reserves. These include John Adams, Thomas Jefferson, John Quincy Adams, Martin Van Buren, Millard Fillmore, Grover Cleveland, William Howard Taft, Woodrow Wilson, Warren Harding, Calvin Coolidge, Herbert Hoover, Franklin D. Roosevelt, and Bill Clinton.

MAKING WAR

Although the president serves as commander in chief, the Constitution does not give the president the power to declare war. This power lies with Congress. The president, however, does have the power to respond if the nation is suddenly attacked, in instances where speed and secrecy might matter.

This has created a number of problems throughout American history. The most obvious is the question of defining what a war is. Presidents have sent American troops into conflict without a congressional declaration of war.

"FREEDOM AT WAR WITH FEAR"

★ ★ ★ ★ ★

On the evening of September 20, 2001, nine days after terrorists attacked the United States, President George W. Bush appeared before a joint session of the House of Representatives and the Senate. His speech entitled "Freedom at War with Fear," would rally and reassure the nation:

> *In the normal course of events, presidents come to this chamber to report on the state of the Union. Tonight, no such report is needed. It has already been delivered by the American people. . . .*
>
> *My fellow citizens, for the last nine days, the entire world has seen for itself the state of our Union—and it is strong. . . .*
>
> *Our response involves far more than instant retaliation and isolated strikes. Americans should not expect one battle, but a lengthy campaign, unlike any other we have ever seen. It may include dramatic strikes, visible on TV, and covert operations, secret even in success. We will starve*

Congress has only declared war for five conflicts—the War of 1812, the Mexican-American War, the Spanish-American War, World War I, and World War II. There are other instances where presidents have sought congressional authorization for the use of military forces; these have included the Vietnam War, the Persian Gulf War, the invasion of Afghanistan following the September 11, 2001, attacks on U.S. soil, and the war in Iraq that began in 2003.

terrorists of funding, turn them one against another, drive them from place to place, until there is no refuge or no rest. And we will pursue nations that provide aid or safe haven to terrorism. Every nation, in every region, now has a decision to make. Either you are with us, or you are with the terrorists. From this day forward, any nation that continues to harbor or support terrorism will be regarded by the United States as a hostile regime. . . .

After all that has just passed—all the lives taken, and all the possibilities and hopes that died with them—it is natural to wonder if America's future is one of fear. Some speak of an age of terror. I know there are struggles ahead, and dangers to face. But this country will define our times, not be defined by them. As long as the United States of America is determined and strong, this will not be an age of terror; this will be an age of liberty, here and across the world. . . .

Presidents do have the power to order the military to stop fighting, and to withdraw from a region in conflict. They have the power to negotiate treaties with an enemy power. If Congress issues an official declaration of war, however, then it must also take some official action to end the state of war between the United States and the other nation. This can happen when the Senate approves—or ratifies—a treaty negotiated by the president to bring a conflict to an end. Congress can also repeal—or declare no longer effective—its declaration of war.

In 1973, Congress passed the War Powers Resolution to ensure that it retained the power to make decisions in matters of war and peace. The passage of this resolution was in response to the Vietnam War; Congress was trying to correct a situation in which Presidents Kennedy, Johnson, and Nixon had been allowed to commit significant numbers of American troops to an expanding war, with little success. The resolution was passed over the veto of President Nixon.

The War Powers Resolution states that the president can commit U.S. armed forces to a situation only after a declaration of war, specific authorization, or a national emergency created by an attack on the United States or its armed forces. The resolution requires the president to inform the House and Senate in writing within 48 hours of any commitment or substantial increase of U.S. combat forces abroad, and it states that the troop commitment must end within 60 days after the president's initial report is submitted unless Congress declares war, specifically approves the continued troop commitment, or is physically unable to meet because of an attack on the United States. Finally, the act also allows Congress to direct the president to remove troops from conflict anytime U.S. forces are involved in combat without a declaration of war or specific congressional approval for military action.

VETO POWER

The word *veto* is from the Latin for "I forbid." The president has the power to veto laws and acts passed by Congress, although the president's veto can be overruled if two-thirds of the members of Congress vote to do so.

According to the Constitution, when Congress passes a bill (an act of legislation) and sends it to the president, he has three possible responses: approve and sign the bill, making it a law; veto (or reject) the bill and return it to the House of Representatives or Senate, whichever it came from, within 10 days; or do nothing. If the president chooses to do nothing, the bill becomes law after 10 days. (If Congress sends a bill to the president and then adjourns before 10 days have passed and before the president has responded, the bill dies. This is called a "pocket veto.")

If the president vetoes a bill, congressional actions determine what happens next. If two-thirds of the members present in both the House and Senate pass the vetoed bill, it becomes law, even though the president has vetoed it. If the House and Senate do not respond, or if not enough members vote to pass the bill, it dies. Congress can then try to rewrite the bill to make it more acceptable to the president or give up on the bill.

Most early presidents used the veto power sparingly, generally only for bills that they felt were unconstitutional. Andrew Jackson was the first president to use the veto as a political weapon against his opponents in Congress. During his time in office, he issued 12 vetoes, more than any president who had come before him.

Party politics were sharp and divisive in the years after the Civil War, and the use of presidential veto power reflected this. Andrew Johnson was the first president whose veto of an important bill was overridden by Congress. In fact, Congress overturned 15 of Johnson's 21 vetoes. These divisions contributed to Johnson's impeachment by the House; he was acquitted in the Senate by only one vote.

President Franklin D. Roosevelt used his veto power against major tax legislation, and he also used the threat of the veto to help him maintain control of many of the laws passed during his presidency. As we read earlier, President Nixon tried to veto the War Powers Resolution that would have limited his ability to commit U.S. forces abroad, but his veto was overridden. The veto power becomes a political tool most often in cases where the president represents one political party and the majority of the members in Congress are of a different political party.

A caricature from the 1830s depicts Andrew Jackson as a tyranni-
cal monarch, holding a scepter in one hand and a "veto" in the other.
Jackson was the first president to use the veto as a political weapon
against opponents in Congress.

THE NATION'S DIPLOMAT

The Constitution grants to the president the power to make treaties (provided that two-thirds of the Senate approves). It also gives the president the power to appoint ambassadors and to receive ambassadors and diplomats from foreign nations.

The president is, in many ways, the most visible representative of the United States to other countries. Modern presidents travel to multiple continents during their terms in office, firming up alliances and trying to build new ones. The president is the official spokesperson for the United States and, because of the powers given to him in the Constitution, he has several different opportunities to influence foreign policy. Through his veto power, he can influence laws related to foreign policy passed by Congress. As commander in chief, he can take—or threaten—military action other than an actual declared war. With the power to appoint ambassadors, the president can choose the men and women who represent the United States overseas. With the power to "receive" (or welcome) foreign ambassadors, the president can choose which countries' representatives he will meet with.

George Washington used treaties rather than personal meetings or agreements with foreign leaders to shape foreign policy; he also consulted Senate leaders to obtain approval before negotiating treaties. Washington was the one who set the precedent that it would be the president who recognized foreign governments—meaning that when a new country was formed, whether through war, revolution,

President George W. Bush is shown talking with Russian President Vladimir Putin during a working session of the G8 Summit in July 2006 in St. Petersburg, Russia. Other world leaders at the session were *(from left)* Prime Minister Junichiro Koizumi of Japan, Prime Minister Stephen Harper of Canada, Prime Minister Matti Vanhanen of Finland, European Commission President José Manuel Barroso, and Prime Minister Romano Prodi of Italy. Because of his position, the president is the most visible representative of the United States.

or overthrow of an existing government, it would be the president who formally recognized it as a new nation. Washington also used his powers to demand that ambassadors be recalled, or sent back to their home countries if they broke U.S. law or committed some offense.

One of Washington's more controversial foreign policy actions was his Neutrality Proclamation of 1793. In it, Washington announced publicly that the United States would remain "friendly and impartial" in the war that had erupted between France and Great Britain. In this case, Congress supported Washington's decision by passing the Neutrality Act of 1794. But many, including Secretary of State Thomas Jefferson, objected to Washington's actions. Their argument was that, if the power to declare war belonged to Congress, then the power to decide that the nation would not engage in war should also belong to Congress.

Presidential control over foreign policy also includes the management of the people within the executive branch whose work is related to foreign affairs. These include the employees of the State Department, the Defense Department, the National Security Agency, the Central Intelligence Agency and all other intelligence agencies, and the Department of Homeland Security.

POLITICAL APPOINTMENTS

Besides the power to appoint ambassadors and consuls, the president also has the power to appoint other political officials who will make decisions and manage many different divisions of the federal government. This is a critical power, one shared to a certain extent with the Senate. The Constitution grants the president the right to name potential appointees; the Senate can either confirm or reject the candidate.

Under the Constitution, the president has the power to select all civilian employees of the federal government whose appointment is not expressly given to other branches of the government. The size of the federal government, however, has dramatically grown since the Constitution was first drafted, with about 2.6 million civilian employees. Today, staff members for the less prominent government positions are recruited and hired by the federal civil service system.

One criticism of presidential appointments is the possibility of patronage, or the system of giving jobs to supporters and friends. Presidential appointments are closely studied, and candidates must be prepared to defend their background, public statements, and qualifications for the job.

When a new president is elected, Congress publishes *Policy and Supporting Positions*, a book that lists the top executive branch positions available for direct presidential appointments. Many of these require Senate confirmation. In general, each new presidential administration is responsible for appointing 200 members of the White House staff, 15 department heads, about 150 ambassadors, as well as many other personnel. Out of these positions, probably about 300 "top jobs"—like members of the president's Cabinet, heads of bureaus, and undersecretaries—are of most concern to the president.

Presidents also have the power to appoint justices to the Supreme Court in the event of a vacancy during their term. This provides the president with an opportunity to influence a separate branch of government—the judicial branch—by placing on the Supreme Court a justice whose positions on legal issues closely reflect those of the president. Supreme Court justices do not serve fixed

Supreme Court Justice Samuel Alito *(left)* was sworn in on February 1, 2006, by Chief Justice John Roberts. Also at the ceremony were *(from left)* Alito's wife, Martha-Ann, and their children, Phil and Laura. Presidents have the power to appoint justices to the Supreme Court, giving them a chance to put their mark on the court long after their term of office has ended. President George W. Bush appointed Roberts and Alito.

terms, nor must they step down when the president who appointed them leaves office. For this reason, Supreme Court appointments offer a president an opportunity to influence the American judicial system well after his administration has ended.

Political appointees are often selected based on their work and educational experience. Previous government service is not a requirement—in fact, many appointees have never worked in the government before. Presidents generally choose candidates who share their vision for that particular office or department and who will demonstrate loyalty to the president. Presidents will also often try to demonstrate balance in their appointments, selecting candidates from different regions of the country, for example. In recent years, presidents have used their appointments to demonstrate a commitment to gender or racial equality. President Lyndon Johnson appointed the first African-American justice to the Supreme Court, Thurgood Marshall, and President Ronald Reagan appointed the first woman justice, Sandra Day O'Connor. Bill Clinton appointed the first woman as secretary of state, Madeleine Albright. George W. Bush appointed the first African-American secretary of state, Colin Powell, and first African-American woman as secretary of state, Condoleezza Rice, named after Powell stepped down.

Although the president has the power to nominate appointees, the Senate retains the power to confirm major presidential appointments. Nominees must supply Senate committees with detailed financial records and undergo background checks, and often nominees are called before Senate committees to answer questions. Although the majority of presidential appointees are confirmed, the Senate does use its power to investigate presidential nominees thoroughly, and, on occasion, nominees are rejected. In recent years, nominees have often asked the president to withdraw their names if it seemed likely that the Senate would not confirm them. The Senate may also use its power to confirm presidential appointments as a negotiating tool to seek presidential support for other policies.

OTHER PRESIDENTIAL POWERS

The president has several powers that are not specifically mentioned in the Constitution but are nonetheless critical to the president's role as the country's chief executive. The president plays a vital role in the shaping of the national budget, often deciding where and how money is spent. While Congress controls national spending, it is the president who prepares and submits a budget for congressional approval.

The president also has the responsibility to ensure that "the Laws be faithfully executed," meaning that he must act as the nation's chief law enforcement official. President John F. Kennedy used this power to order U.S. marshals (and later federal troops) to Oxford, Mississippi, to provide federal support for a court order requiring the University of Mississippi to enroll an African-American student, James Meredith, in 1962. The marshals and troops were sent to maintain order on the campus and to protect Meredith.

The law enforcement power also places the president at the head of federal law enforcement agencies, including the Federal Bureau of Investigation, the Office of Citizenship and Immigration Services, the Drug Enforcement Administration, and the U.S. Marshals Service. The Justice Department is the president's principal law enforcement agency. Investigations and law enforcement also may be carried out by the Food and Drug Administration, U.S.

Customs and Border Protection, the Secret Service, and the Internal Revenue Service. Other areas of federal law enforcement are carried out by the Labor Department, the Occupational Safety and Health Administration, the Federal Aviation Administration, and the Coast Guard.

4

INSIDE THE
OVAL OFFICE

The Oval Office is the president's office, and when he is at the White House, the Oval Office is the heart of presidential business. The Oval Office is not a historic part of the presidency—in fact, the entire West Wing of the White House, where the Oval Office is located, is little more than 100 years old—but the idea of a round or oval room for the president dates back to the time of George Washington.

It was Washington who began the practice of holding gatherings in an oval room. In his home in Philadelphia, where the capital was then located, Washington altered two rooms to make them oval, and he would hold formal receptions there. Washington would stand in the center of the room, with guests gathered around him in a circle. The idea was to ensure that there was no top or bottom, no head or foot, to the room, so that everyone could be an equal distance from the president.

John Adams was the first president to occupy the White House, at the time called the "President's House," when the capital relocated to Washington, D.C., from Philadelphia. The building was not finished when Adams moved into it in 1800. Thirteen fires had to be kept burning constantly to help speed up the drying of paint and plaster, and only six of the building's 30 rooms were completed. Adams's wife, Abigail, hung her laundry to dry in the large, unfinished reception room.

For many years, presidents lived and worked on the second floor of the White House. President Theodore Roosevelt, however, found the living quarters on the second floor too cramped for his large family, and he decided to have new working space built in a separate building on the west side of the White House. At the time, the White House's greenhouses were in this area, but in 1902 these were moved to make way for the new office space.

The Oval Office in the West Wing was the idea of President William Howard Taft, who in 1909 decided that the president's office should be in the center of the West Wing. Taft wanted to ensure that the president was at the center of all West Wing operations and involved in all of the day-to-day activities of the presidency. The Oval Office was moved to its current location—next to the Rose Garden—under President Franklin D. Roosevelt.

President George W. Bush held a meeting on December 20, 2001, in the Oval Office, which was decorated with the new presidential rug that arrived earlier in the week. Presidents choose the design for the rug in the Oval Office, though all rugs feature the great seal of the United States in the center.

In many ways, the Oval Office has become a symbol of the American presidency. Photos of the president frequently show him in the Oval Office; the president may deliver important speeches from behind his desk in the Oval Office.

Tradition dictates that each president chooses the decor of the Oval Office, and interesting glimpses into the presidential character—into the people he admires and his vision for the country—can be seen in how he chooses to decorate his office. President Taft's Oval Office was decorated in olive green, with caribou hides tacked with gold studs on the chairs and a wooden floor with a checkerboard pattern.

In more recent years, the floor of the Oval Office has been covered with a large rug, whose design is chosen by each president. President George W. Bush chose a sunny, optimistic yellow to decorate the Oval Office, with a rug designed to mimic the sunlight flowing in through the large windows looking out onto the South Lawn of the White House. The presidential rugs all feature the great seal of the United States in their center. The eagle depicted in the seal holds an olive branch in one of its talons and several arrows in the other. Today, the eagle's head is turned toward the olive branch, although it used to face the arrows. This change was made by President Harry Truman after World War II, to demonstrate that the United States would now be looking toward peace rather than war.

The desk in the Oval Office is also chosen by the president. Many recent presidents have selected the desk known as "HMS Resolute," including Theodore and Franklin D. Roosevelt, Ronald Reagan, Bill Clinton, and John F. Kennedy. The desk, a gift from Queen Victoria to President Rutherford Hayes in 1879, was made of timbers from the British ship HMS *Resolute*. This desk had originally been open in the front, but a panel was added by Franklin D. Roosevelt to hide the fact that his legs were crippled by polio.

The artwork in the Oval Office also reflects the spirit and focus of the man whose office it has become. Presidents

President Bill Clinton sits at his desk, known as the "HMS Resolute," in the Oval Office. With him at the January 23, 1993, meeting was Robert Rubin, chairman of the National Economic Council. HMS Resolute has been used by many presidents, including Ronald Reagan and John F. Kennedy.

often choose portraits or busts of former presidents whose leadership inspires them.

These items are what a visitor to the Oval Office might see. But more important than the look of the Oval Office is the work conducted there.

THE PRESIDENT'S MEN AND WOMEN

The tradition of selecting a "cabinet," or collection of advisors, dates back to the very first president. George Washington's cabinet included Secretary of the Treasury Alexander Hamilton, Secretary of State Thomas Jefferson, Attorney General Edmund Randolph, and Secretary of War Henry Knox. They, along with Vice President John Adams, formed the entire executive branch of government in 1789.

Today, the president's cabinet has considerably expanded. Presidents are given the opportunity to add cabinet positions. The modern presidential cabinet includes the vice president, the attorney general (who is the head of the Justice Department), and the heads of 14 other departments—Agriculture, Commerce, Defense, Education, Energy, Health and Human Services, Homeland Security, Housing and Urban Development, Interior, Labor, State, Transportation, Treasury, and Veterans Affairs. In recent years, the administrator of the Environmental Protection Agency, the director of the Office of Management and Budget, the director of the Office of National Drug Control Policy, and the U.S. trade representative have been elevated to cabinet-level rank. Presidents choose the men and women who will serve in their cabinet, based upon the approval of the Senate.

Because the federal government has grown so large and its responsibilities so vast, the president must in many ways act as a kind of chief administrator, directing the activities of the various departments through his instructions to the cabinet members. For this reason, the cabinet members may offer the president advice or make recommendations, but they serve at the president's request and are expected to carry out his programs or orders.

The president cannot possibly know every detail of what goes on in each office within the executive branch. He may have a broad vision for that office—for example, he may have an idea of how he wants the secretary of state to respond to a particular incident in a foreign country—but in essence a key to a successful presidency involves skilled delegation. The president is, in many ways, a manager, and successful presidents choose skilled men and women to serve them and wisely delegate enough so that they can focus and concentrate on their priorities as president.

THE COMMUNICATOR

The president relies on the heads of departments, and on his staff, to keep him informed of developments critical to his administration and to the nation's security and stability. It is the president, however, who is the chief communicator for his administration; he is periodically expected to communicate his policies and decisions to Congress and to the nation.

President George W. Bush handed copies of his address to Speaker of the House Dennis Hastert *(left)* and Vice President Dick Cheney at the start of his State of the Union on January 31, 2006. The State of the Union speech has become a ceremonial event for presidents and Congress.

The Constitution provides for the president to "from time to time give to the Congress Information of the State of the Union." The State of the Union speech has become an annual event, giving the president the opportunity to address the Congress (and the American public, since the speeches are generally televised) and to outline his broad plans for the future, as well as to review what has been accomplished in the last 12 months.

The custom of appearing in person before the Congress to inform its members of the "State of the Union" began with George Washington and was continued by John Adams, both of whom appeared each year to deliver a message in person to Congress. Thomas Jefferson, believing this practice had too much in common with the custom of the British Parliament beginning its session with a speech from the king or queen, decided to put a stop to it. Jefferson preferred to submit his reports to Congress in writing.

Jefferson's custom of a written "State of the Union" report was continued until 1913, when Woodrow Wilson personally appeared before Congress to deliver a special speech on finance. This marked not only a return to the personal delivery of the State of the Union report in a speech, but also the beginning of the use of the speech as a way to publicize the president's plans and agenda. This idea became more pronounced when the speeches were broadcast on radio and, of course, on television.

Presidents have used the State of the Union speech to bring new ideas and programs to the public attention. President Kennedy used his State of the Union speech to urge support for the effort to put a man on the moon before the end of the 1960s. Lyndon Johnson used his State of the Union speeches to urge passage of his civil rights programs, while President Nixon used his to try to gain public support for U.S. actions in Vietnam.

The State of the Union speech has become a ceremonial event for the presidency and for Congress. Among those in the audience are members of the Joint Chiefs of Staff (the highest-ranking member of each branch of the armed services), the president's cabinet, justices of the Supreme Court, and certain invited guests. Presidents may use the speech to recognize a private individual for some heroic act, to remind the audience of successful accomplishments, and to gain support for their political party.

Through the years, presidents have used other tools to communicate their proposals and agendas. The presidential staff normally includes several speechwriters and a press secretary, who provides reporters with daily briefings, advance texts and reports, and announcements of the president's schedule and new policies.

Presidents may hold periodic news conferences to make policy announcements and answer reporters' questions. This custom began with Woodrow Wilson, who was the first president to invite reporters to his office for a question-and-answer session. Before this, presidents had usually granted interviews only to certain reporters, generally those who would report favorably on the administration. Franklin D. Roosevelt proved a master at the press conference, often holding them twice a week and entertaining reporters with his lively responses and charm. Dwight Eisenhower was the first to allow his news conferences to be televised, although he reserved the right to edit them before they were presented to the public. With his successor, John F. Kennedy, the press conferences were no longer edited.

Presidents engage in extensive preparation before press conferences, working with their staff to guess which questions will be asked and to prepare careful responses. The frequency of presidential news conferences can reflect the

THE "GREAT SOCIETY" SPEECH

★ ★ ★ ★ ★

It is the responsibility of each president to critically examine the country he leads, to carefully measure its strengths and weaknesses, and to provide leadership that will inspire. In 1964, President Lyndon Johnson chose a theme for his administration: the "Great Society." Johnson communicated this new plan for the nation at a May 1964 commencement address at the University of Michigan:

> . . . *The purpose of protecting the life of our nation and preserving the liberty of our citizens is to pursue the happiness of our people. Our success in that pursuit is the test of our success as a nation. For a century we labored to settle and to subdue a continent. For half a century, we called upon unbounded invention and untiring industry to create an order of plenty for all of our people. The challenge of the next half century is whether we have the wisdom to use that wealth to enrich and elevate our national life, and to advance the quality of our American civilization.*
>
> *Your imagination, your initiative, and your indignation will determine whether we build a society where progress is the servant of our needs, or a society where old values and new visions are buried under unbridled growth.*

president's ease at dealing with unanticipated questions or a possibly hostile questioner, and when administrations are dealing with crises, the number of press conferences often dwindles.

For in your time we have the opportunity to move not only toward the rich society and the powerful society, but upward to the Great Society. The Great Society rests on abundance and liberty for all. It demands an end to poverty and racial injustice, to which we are totally committed in our time. But that is just the beginning.

The Great Society is a place where every child can find knowledge to enrich his mind and to enlarge his talents. It is a place where leisure is a welcome chance to build and reflect, not a feared cause of boredom and restlessness. It is a place where the city of man serves not only the needs of the body and the demands of commerce, but the desire for beauty and the hunger for community.

It is a place where man can renew contact with nature. It is a place which honors creation for its own sake and for what it adds to the understanding of the race. It is a place where men are more concerned with the quality of their goals than the quantity of their goods. But most of all, the Great Society is not a safe harbor, a resting place, a final objective, a finished work. It is a challenge constantly renewed, beckoning us toward a destiny where the meaning of our lives matches the marvelous products of our labor. . . .

Journalists peppered President Franklin D. Roosevelt *(seated, right)* with questions during a news conference held at his estate in Hyde Park, New York, in August 1933. Roosevelt proved to be a master of the news conference, often holding them twice a week.

Instead, presidents may rely on more structured opportunities to present their policies to the public. They may make speeches before carefully screened audiences; they may give televised "addresses" or speeches during which reporters do not have an opportunity to ask questions; or they may grant interviews only to reporters with whom they have established a friendly relationship.

5

ELECTING THE
PRESIDENT

The details of the election of a president, and how he leaves office, are spelled out in the Constitution. The framers of the Constitution, though, could not have imagined the wild excesses of a presidential campaign or the many variables that have led to a president leaving office.

In the very first election, George Washington was the unanimous choice of the electors. Each elector had to name two choices on the ballot for president, and each gave one of his votes to Washington. At the time, the candidate who came in second became vice president. In that first election, John Adams became vice president.

In the future, such agreement in the choice of president would prove rare. In the early years of the United

States, men who were instrumental in the shaping of the new nation's government would become its leaders—men like Washington and Adams, Thomas Jefferson, and James Madison. Future generations, though, would need to find other ways to select the man (for until now it has always been a man) who would become president. And the process of choosing a president would become increasingly complex.

THE ELECTORAL COLLEGE

When creating the Constitution, the delegates to the Constitutional Convention considered several ways to elect a president. They considered and rejected the idea that Congress would choose the president. They considered and rejected the idea that the legislatures of each state would choose the president. They also considered and rejected the idea that a president would be directly elected by the people. The problems with the first two options are clear, but why did the framers of the Constitution reject the last option?

It is important to remember that, at the time, the population of the 13 states was widely scattered, and there were no quick means of communication connecting the states. The delegates feared that the voters would not easily be able to find out much information about the different candidates for the presidency. Without this kind of information, they would probably vote for the candidate with whom they were familiar, most likely the candidate from their state or region. This would give an advantage to candidates from the more heavily populated and larger states.

To create a more balanced system, the framers of the Constitution came up with the idea of an "Electoral College." The idea was that well-informed people would be selected from each state to cast their vote for the best presidential candidate. The number of voters, or delegates to the Electoral College, is based on the number of congressional representatives each state has. So clearly there is an advantage for larger, more populated states, which will have more votes to cast in the Electoral College.

The Constitution contains the details of what would become the first Electoral College. In it, each state was given two electoral votes (one for each senator) plus one vote for each member of the House of Representatives. Each state could decide how its electors would be chosen, but congressmen and employees of the federal government could not serve as electors. Each elector had to cast two votes for president, and one of those votes had to be for someone who was not from their home state. The person with the most electoral votes (and it had to be more than one-half of the votes) would become president. If no one received more than one-half of the votes or if there was a tie, the election would be decided by the House of Representatives. Members of the House would review the top five candidates, and each state would be allowed to cast only one vote. The president would need to receive more than one-half of all the votes cast.

This system worked for only four presidential elections. In the election of 1800, Thomas Jefferson and Aaron Burr received an equal number of votes. It took many days and 36 separate voting sessions (plus a lot of behind-the-scenes deal-making) before the House of Representatives finally resolved the election in favor of Jefferson.

This led to the ratification of the Twelfth Amendment to the Constitution in 1804. In it, the rules were changed so that each elector would cast one vote for president and a separate vote for vice president, rather than the previous system of casting two votes for president. According to the amendment, if no one receives more than one-half of the votes, then the House of Representatives chooses the president from the top three contenders, with each state casting only one vote. The amendment also specified that either the president or vice president had to be from a state other than that of the electors. This is why modern presidential and vice-presidential candidates are always from different states.

Today, most states choose their electors by statewide election. And most follow a "winner take all" system. This means that the presidential candidate who wins the popular vote in a state receives all of that state's electors. It is interesting to note that when a citizen casts his vote in a presidential election, he is not directly voting for that presidential candidate, but instead for the *electors* for the presidential candidate he has chosen.

During the first presidential elections, states were given the right to choose their electors on whatever date they

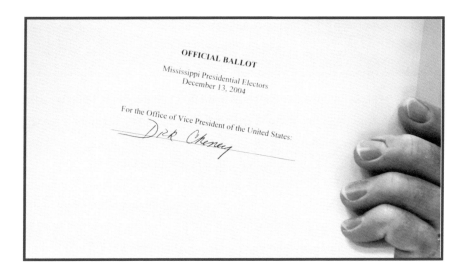

This ballot for vice president, one of six cast by the Electoral College participants from Mississippi in 2004, shows the name of Vice President Dick Cheney. Most states today choose their electors for the Electoral College by statewide election, and most follow a "winner take all" system.

fixed. In 1845, Congress passed a law specifying that all states would choose their electors on the same day—the Tuesday following the first Monday in November in years that can be divided by four. That day remains the day on which presidential elections are held.

PROBLEMS WITH ELECTING THE PRESIDENT
The election of 1800 was not the only time that the system devised for choosing a president caused trouble. In 1824, the electoral votes were split among four strong candidates—John Quincy Adams, Andrew Jackson, Henry

CAMP DAVID

Presidents seeking a retreat from the White House, and a more informal setting at which to relax and meet with staff members or guests, can travel to Camp David, some 70 miles from Washington in the Catoctin Mountains of Maryland.

President Franklin D. Roosevelt first established Camp David on the site of a camp for federal workers and their families. Roosevelt drew up the plans for the construction of a main lodge and improvements to many of the cabins on the grounds; he called it "Shangri-La" and was the first president to use the camp during a three-day retreat in 1942. He also played host to the first foreign official there—Prime Minister Winston Churchill of Great Britain in 1943.

President Dwight Eisenhower renamed the retreat Camp David in honor of his grandson, David Eisenhower. Eisenhower held the first cabinet meeting at Camp David.

The retreat has served as the site of important meetings and summits. In 1978, President Jimmy Carter conducted Middle East peace negotiations with Israel's Menachem Begin and Egypt's Anwar Sadat in what became known as the Camp David Accords.

President Ronald Reagan spent more time at Camp David than any other president. President George H.W. Bush's daughter, Dorothy, was married there. Besides privacy and cooler temperatures, Camp David offers a pool, a putting green, a driving range, tennis courts, and a workout center. The president normally travels to Camp David by helicopter.

Clay, and William Crawford. No one received a clear majority (more than one-half) of the votes, and it fell to the House of Representatives to choose the president. Andrew Jackson had received more electoral votes than any of the other three contenders, but the House narrowly selected John Quincy Adams as president.

In 1876, the election was between Samuel Tilden and Rutherford Hayes. Most counts showed that Tilden had won the majority of the popular vote, but the electoral votes in South Carolina, Louisiana, and Florida were in question. In the end, each state provided two sets of electoral votes, one for Tilden and one for Hayes. Congress appointed a 15-member commission to decide the electoral votes in each of the three states. There were charges of political deal-making and behind-the-scenes negotiations, but in the end the commission narrowly chose Hayes as the winner of the electoral votes in each of the three states, and he was elected president. In 1887, Congress passed a law giving each state the final authority to determine whether its electoral votes were legal.

In 1888, the election between Benjamin Harrison and Grover Cleveland demonstrated how a candidate could win the popular vote and still lose the election. Benjamin Harrison, the Republican candidate, barely won majorities in some of the larger of the 20 states that supported him, while in the 18 states that supported him, Cleveland won huge majorities of the popular vote. In the overall popular vote, Cleveland surpassed Harrison 5,534,488 to

5,443,892. Nonetheless, the candidate who won the majority of electoral votes—in this case, Benjamin Harrison (233 to 168)—was elected president.

In more recent history, the 2000 presidential election demonstrated the significance of electoral votes in one of the closest elections in history. On election night, many television networks prematurely announced a winner in the election, before it was decided that the results were too close to call. The election came down to the 25 electoral votes of the state of Florida. When it was learned that Republican candidate George W. Bush had won by only a little more than 1,000 votes in Florida over Democratic challenger Al Gore, a recount of the votes was ordered. It took nearly a month of court challenges and recounts before the U.S. Supreme Court finally intervened, stating that each Florida county was using different vote-counting standards and there was insufficient time to create a single standard and appoint an impartial official to oversee the recounts. The election was awarded to George W. Bush; the disputed final results show Bush winning Florida's electors by only 537 votes.

PRIMARIES AND CAUCUSES

The creation of political parties and the vast media attention devoted to presidential elections has transformed the process of choosing the president. Today, candidates must raise vast amounts of money to support a political campaign, and the process of attracting public attention (and campaign contributions) begins well before the national election. Generally, candidates declare their intention to run for the presidency at least a year before the national election is held.

The first goal that candidates face is to win their political party's nomination for the general election at a nominating convention held the summer before the general election. To become the Democratic or Republican candidate for president, a candidate must be nominated at the Democratic Party's or the Republican Party's convention. Since there may be more than one candidate from the party seeking to become president, primaries and caucuses are held to give voters the opportunity to register their support for a particular candidate before the nominating convention is held.

Primaries began in the early part of the twentieth century. Before this, candidates for each party were, for the most part, chosen by party insiders, who made deals and traded favors while selecting the candidate they thought would be most likely to win a presidential election.

In some states, only voters who are registered to a particular party can vote for that party's candidate in a primary—for example, only registered Republicans can vote for the Republican candidate. In other states, voters can vote for another party's candidate.

The nomination of presidential candidates generally involves either primaries or caucuses, depending on the state's rules. A primary resembles a general election—voters go to

A supporter of John Kerry offered last-minute advice at a caucus site in Des Moines, Iowa, in January 2004. Primaries and caucuses are held to give voters the chance to choose who they want to run for president as the Republican or Democratic nominee.

a polling place and cast their vote for a particular candidate. In a caucus, party members gather together in a public place and often listen to speeches before casting their votes for delegates to represent a particular candidate at the party's national convention.

Within each state, Republican and Democratic primaries and caucuses are held at the same time, but the date when these votes occur varies from state to state. This happens between January and June of an election year. One criticism of this system is that states that hold the first primaries and caucuses—Iowa and New Hampshire—receive a large amount of attention from the candidates and the media, attention that does not necessarily reflect the number of electoral votes they will ultimately cast for president. Candidates who do not perform well in the earlier primaries and caucuses may have to drop out before the primaries and caucuses have ended, meaning that states that hold their primaries and caucuses first have a greater opportunity to influence the ultimate choice of presidential candidate. Many states, including New York, Ohio, and California (with large numbers of electoral votes), hold their primaries on the same Tuesday in March, which has become known as "Super Tuesday."

The primaries and caucuses decide how many delegates for each candidate will be sent to the national convention. At the national convention, the delegates from each state then vote for the candidate they wish to receive the party's nomination. The winner is selected as the party's official candidate for president.

THE CAMPAIGN

Once the parties have chosen their candidates for president, these nominees spend the next several months demonstrating to the voters why they would be the best president. In the country's early years, many candidates believed that it was undignified to express an interest in becoming president. They felt that they should seem to be above the election process, leaving the campaigning and negotiations to their supporters.

The campaign provides an opportunity to present the candidate to the voters, highlighting certain strengths and types of experience, and focusing on specific issues. Throughout the years, campaigns have highlighted the candidates' positions on the economy, on defense, on civil rights, and on a wide range of other issues that reflect the concerns of voters at a particular time.

Campaigns have traditionally not only highlighted a particular candidate's strengths but also an opponent's weaknesses. Even candidates like John Adams and Thomas Jefferson inspired fierce criticism. In the 1800 presidential election, voters were warned of the dangers of re-electing Adams with posters that proclaimed, "REPUBLICANS, Turn out, turn out and save your Country from ruin!"

Campaigns frequently focus on a candidate's background. In the nineteenth century, a candidate's humble beginnings were considered an asset, and many presidential candidates emphasized their births in log cabins and their time spent on the frontier. Campaigns might emphasize a candidate's war service or his political experience, or link him to other popular figures. In recent years, it has been considered a liability, rather than an asset, to have spent too much of a career in Washington, and candidates who have served as U.S. senators or representatives will frequently have their campaigns focus on other aspects of their background.

President George W. Bush and Democratic challenger John Kerry debated in St. Louis in October 2004, a month before the election. Presidential debates were first televised in 1960, when John F. Kennedy and Richard Nixon were running for president.

Television has also dramatically changed the presidential campaign process. Now campaigns focus on televised appearances by the candidate to present a particular issue or position to the voters. Appearance matters—candidates who appear poised and confident in front of the cameras are much more likely to win the election. This was first proved in the 1960 presidential election, the first in which debates between the two presidential candidates were televised. Polls showed that voters who had listened to the debates on the radio thought that Republican candidate Richard Nixon had won, but television viewers strongly favored Democratic candidate John F. Kennedy, who appeared relaxed, attractive, and confident on camera. Kennedy ultimately won the presidential election.

6

PRESIDENTIAL TRANSITIONS

In most cases, a candidate becomes president after an election. There is an orderly transition after four or eight years (depending on whether a president is re-elected).

There have been occasions, however, when a president was unable to serve his full term. Presidents have died after illnesses, have been killed, and have resigned.

There is a specific plan in place should the president be unable to complete his term in office. The order of who succeeds the president has changed over the years. The order of succession spelled out in the Presidential Succession Act of 1947, signed by President Harry Truman, is still in effect today.

Should the president be unable to complete his term, he will be succeeded by the vice president. If the vice president is also unable to serve, people in the following offices (in this order) will become president, provided that they meet the constitutional requirements for the presidency (at least 35 years old, a natural-born citizen of the United States, and a U.S. resident for at least 14 years): Speaker of the House, president pro tempore of the Senate (the senator who presides over the Senate when the vice president is absent), secretary of state, secretary of the treasury, secretary of defense, attorney general, secretary of the interior, secretary of agriculture, secretary of commerce, secretary of labor, secretary of health and human services, secretary of housing and urban development, secretary of transportation, secretary of energy, secretary of education, secretary of veterans affairs, and secretary of homeland security.

DEATH IN OFFICE

A president has died in office after an illness four times. The shortest presidential term in history is that of William Henry Harrison, who died in 1841, only one month after becoming president. Harrison was 68 years old, but many suggest that Harrison's inaugural address was to blame for his death. The day of his inauguration was bitterly cold, and Harrison was outside for nearly two hours delivering the longest inaugural speech in history. Harrison caught a cold, which developed into pneumonia, and he died.

Zachary Taylor served from 1849 to 1850. He became ill after participating in a ceremony on a blisteringly hot

William Henry Harrison, who died just a month after his inauguration, had the shortest presidency on record. He is also known, however, for making the longest inaugural address in history.

July 4 at the Washington Monument, which was still under construction. Within five days, he was dead, succeeded by Millard Fillmore.

Warren Harding served from 1921 to 1923. Corruption and scandals had already weakened his administration when Harding set out on a western tour in the summer of 1923. He collapsed in San Francisco and died of a heart attack.

Franklin D. Roosevelt remains the longest-serving president. He was elected to four terms but died before completing his last term. Roosevelt served from 1933 to 1945. His health had been poor for many of his last years in office, and he died of a brain hemorrhage on April 12, 1945.

ASSASSINATIONS

As a public symbol of the United States, the president receives tremendous attention. Presidents inspire strong emotions, both admiration and hatred. It is perhaps not surprising that presidents may become targets for attack. The Secret Service is charged with protecting the president and his family from these attacks, but assassination attempts have been made on several presidents. In four cases, presidents were killed.

Presidents Andrew Jackson, Theodore Roosevelt, Franklin Roosevelt, Harry Truman, Gerald Ford, and Ronald Reagan were the victims of attempted assassinations. In Jackson's case, the guns misfired. Theodore Roosevelt and Reagan were wounded but survived. In Franklin Roosevelt's case, the bullets missed him but killed the mayor of Chicago and wounded several other people. Similarly, the attempt on Truman left him unhurt, but a guard died and two others were wounded. Gerald Ford survived two assassination attempts within a three-week period. No one was injured in the attempts.

President Abraham Lincoln was the first president to be assassinated while in office. Lincoln died on April 15, 1865, after being shot by John Wilkes Booth while attending a performance at Ford's Theatre in Washington.

President James Garfield was shot on July 2, 1881, at a Washington railroad station by an attorney who had unsuccessfully sought a diplomatic position. Garfield lay wounded at the White House for several weeks and then was moved to the New Jersey coast. It was probably poor medical care that contributed to Garfield's death—he died on September 19, 1881, from an infection and internal bleeding.

William McKinley served as president from 1897 to 1901. He was shot by a crazed opponent of his policies while standing in a receiving line in Buffalo and died eight days later.

President John F. Kennedy was also the victim of assassination. He was shot and killed on November 22, 1963, while traveling in a motorcade through the streets of Dallas, Texas.

IMPEACHMENT

The Constitution specifies that presidents can face impeachment and be removed from office if they are convicted of "Treason, Bribery, or other high Crimes and Misdemeanors." Only two presidents have undergone impeachment trials: Andrew Johnson in 1868 and Bill Clinton in 1999.

AIR FORCE ONE

The presidential transportation known as Air Force One is actually two planes: specially designed Boeing 747 aircraft that are capable of flying halfway around the world without refueling and can accommodate up to 70 passengers. When the president is aboard either plane—or any Air Force aircraft—its call sign automatically becomes "Air Force One."

President Franklin D. Roosevelt was the first to call for the creation of what became known as the Presidential Pilot Office to provide air transportation for the president and his staff in 1944. The first jet aircraft—a Boeing 707—was purchased in 1962.

Air Force One functions as a traveling office for the president and his staff. Onboard, they have access to secure phone, fax, and computer lines, as well as copiers and printers. The president has his own office onboard, as well as a bedroom, a bathroom, and a dining room that is also used as a conference room. Senior staff members have their own office space, and there is a separate seating area for reporters traveling with the president.

A crew of 26 people serves onboard Air Force One. Because the two Air Force One jets are military aircraft, they are built to withstand air attacks. They also have in-flight refueling connections; the jets do not need to land to refuel.

In order for a president to be removed from office, there must first be a formal accusation in the House of Representatives and then an impeachment trial and conviction

In this photo from the U.S. Senate, Chief Justice William H. Rehnquist swore in the U.S. senators as jurors in January 1999 in the impeachment trial of President Bill Clinton. A two-thirds majority of senators must vote to convict in an impeachment trial; Clinton was not convicted.

in the Senate. A majority vote (more than half of the votes) is required for the House to order an impeachment, but a two-thirds majority is necessary for the Senate to convict a president. In the event of an impeachment trial, the chief justice of the Supreme Court presides over the Senate.

In the cases of Johnson and Clinton, there were not enough votes to convict in the Senate. Both men remained in office.

Richard Nixon says goodbye to his staff members outside the White House as he boards a helicopter after resigning the presidency. Nixon stepped down on August 9, 1974, to avoid an impeachment trial in which he would probably have been convicted.

RESIGNATION

President Richard Nixon was the first and only president to resign his office. Nixon resigned to avoid facing an impeachment trial, a trial that would probably have resulted in his conviction.

Shortly after Nixon's re-election in 1972, his administration became involved in the Watergate scandal, which involved a break-in at the offices of the Democratic National Committee at the Watergate hotel complex. The break-in was traced to members of Nixon's re-election committee. Ultimately, it was revealed that Nixon had known of the involvement and had tried to cover it up. Nixon resigned on August 9, 1974, and was succeeded by Gerald Ford.

Ford had been appointed by Nixon in 1973, after the resignation of Nixon's first vice president, Spiro Agnew. Upon becoming president, Ford appointed Nelson Rockefeller as his vice president. For the 29 months that Ford served as president, the country was run by a president and vice president who had not been elected to the offices they held.

7

WHO WANTS TO BE PRESIDENT?

HELP WANTED for senior government position. Must be willing to undergo rigorous screening process and challenging campaign season. Must be able to commit to position for at least four years, with possibility of additional four years. Successful candidate must be at least 35 years old, a U.S. citizen, and have lived in the country for at least 14 years. Military service and fund-raising skills helpful, but not required.

Responsibilities include: representing country at home and overseas; meeting with major world leaders; negotiating treaties; shaping policy; serving as commander in chief of the armed forces; preparing annual budget; appointing ambassadors, justices of the Supreme Court, and other specified public officials. Must prepare annual progress report to be delivered to Congress.

Benefits include housing and transportation, bodyguards for personal protection, plus use of jet, vacation retreat, and expense account for office staff, entertaining, and travel. Salary: $400,000 per year. Must be willing to relocate to Washington, D.C.

If a want ad were created for the job of president of the United States, it might look something like this. The salary is impressive, the benefits are exceptional, and yet the responsibilities are overwhelming. The job can prove physically and mentally exhausting. Look at pictures of presidents when they first enter the office and then when they leave, four or eight years later—the weight of the office is clearly visible in the way they have aged over a relatively short period of time.

According to *The American Heritage History of the Presidency* by Marcus Cunliffe, John Adams reportedly said as he was nearing the end of his life, "No man who ever held the office of president would congratulate a friend on obtaining it." And yet, every few years many prominent people declare their intent to run for the presidency.

Who is most likely to win the election? What qualifications and experience are most likely to provide a candidate with the background to become the president of the United States?

THE BASICS

When you review pictures of the presidents of the United States, two facts quickly become clear. First, they have all been men. Second, they have all been white.

There is no requirement in the Constitution that specifies race or gender of the president. At least 21 women have tried to become president, 15 by seeking the nomination of either the Democratic or Republican parties. The first woman to seek the presidency was Victoria Woodhull, who was a candidate of the Equal Rights Party in 1872. In 1984, the Democratic Party named a woman, Geraldine Ferraro, as its candidate for the vice presidency. She and her running mate, presidential candidate Walter Mondale, lost the election to Ronald Reagan.

That same year, African-American activist Jesse Jackson ran for the Democratic Party nomination. He was not the first black candidate for president. Shirley Chisholm had run for the Democratic Party nomination in 1972, and other African Americans have run for president on third-party tickets and have sought the nomination of the two major parties in more recent elections.

It seems certain that the presidency will become more diverse—in terms of gender and race—in the near future. As the "stepping stones" to the presidency become more diverse, the presidency will as well. What are these "stepping stones"—the jobs that tend to produce the most

Elected in 1968, Shirley Chisholm was the first African-American woman to serve in Congress. Four years later, she became the first African-American woman to make a serious bid for a major-party presidential nomination. She ultimately lost the Democratic nomination to George McGovern.

presidents? And what common traits and experiences do most presidents share?

WORKING TOWARD THE PRESIDENCY

More than two-thirds of all presidents have been college graduates, although a college degree has not always been necessary to win the presidency. Nine presidents never attended college: George Washington, Andrew Jackson, Martin Van Buren, Zachary Taylor,

Millard Fillmore, Abraham Lincoln, Andrew Johnson, Grover Cleveland, and Harry Truman. Harvard University has the honor of having the most presidents—six—as alumni: John Adams, John Quincy Adams, Theodore Roosevelt, Franklin Roosevelt, John Kennedy, and George W. Bush (who attended Harvard Business School). Yale is in second place, with five presidents as alumni: William Taft, Gerald Ford (law school), George H.W. Bush, Bill Clinton (law school), and George W. Bush (undergraduate).

Most (but not all) presidents have had some political experience before their election. Fourteen presidents served first as vice presidents: John Adams, Thomas Jefferson, Martin Van Buren, John Tyler, Millard Fillmore, Andrew Johnson, Chester Arthur, Theodore Roosevelt, Calvin Coolidge, Harry Truman, Lyndon Johnson, Richard Nixon, Gerald Ford, and George H.W. Bush. Others have served as Cabinet officers, ambassadors, or members of the House of Representatives or Senate.

Nineteen presidents have served as governors of states or territories. Six were governor when they became president (Rutherford Hayes, Grover Cleveland, Woodrow Wilson, Franklin Roosevelt, Bill Clinton, and George W. Bush). Only one mayor of a large city—Grover Cleveland, who had been mayor of Buffalo before he was governor of New York—has ever become president.

More than two-thirds of all presidents have had training in the law. Three had no political experience and were elected because of their service as Army generals—Zachary Taylor, Ulysses Grant, and Dwight Eisenhower. Herbert Hoover never ran for any elected office before becoming president, although he had served as secretary of commerce and with several national and international relief agencies during World War I.

Ten presidents served as elementary or secondary school teachers—John Adams, Andrew Jackson, Millard Fillmore, Franklin Pierce, James Garfield, Chester Arthur, Grover Cleveland (at a school for the deaf), William McKinley, Warren Harding, and Lyndon Johnson. Five presidents taught at colleges or graduate schools—John Quincy Adams, James Garfield, William Taft, Woodrow Wilson, and Bill Clinton.

Many presidents, particularly in the early years of the presidency, owned farms or plantations. No doctors or ministers have been elected to the presidency, although William Henry Harrison briefly studied medicine and both John Adams and James Madison studied religion.

Another common trait of many presidents is personal wealth. Herbert Hoover, Lyndon Johnson, Franklin Roosevelt, and John Kennedy were all millionaires. Thomas Jefferson was the only president to die in debt; James Madison and James Monroe were living close to poverty at the end of their lives.

Most presidents come from small towns or rural areas. Only five were born in large cities, and several (including Andrew Jackson, James Polk, Millard Fillmore, James

Buchanan, Abraham Lincoln, and James Garfield) spent their childhoods living in a log cabin.

The average age of a president at his inauguration is 54. Ronald Reagan was the oldest, inaugurated to his

PRESIDENTIAL TRIVIA

1. How many presidents have served a single term or less?

    a. Five
    b. Thirteen
    c. Eighteen
    d. Twenty-two

2. Which president served as chief justice of the Supreme Court after his presidency ended?

    a. Andrew Johnson
    b. John Adams
    c. William Taft
    d. Warren Harding

3. Which president served as director of the Central Intelligence Agency?

    a. George H.W. Bush
    b. John Kennedy
    c. Richard Nixon
    d. Millard Fillmore

first term only a few weeks before his seventieth birthday. John Kennedy was the youngest to be elected president, at age 43, but Theodore Roosevelt was the youngest man to *become* president. He was 42 years old

4. Who was the only president to marry at the White House?

    a. Bill Clinton
    b. Grover Cleveland
    c. Thomas Jefferson
    d. Lyndon Johnson

5. Which president worked as a movie actor before pursuing a career in politics?

    a. John Kennedy
    b. George W. Bush
    c. Ronald Reagan
    d. Gerald Ford

ANSWERS: 1. d; 2. c; 3. a; 4. b; 5. c

President Ronald Reagan kissed his wife, Nancy, just after being
sworn in as the fortieth U.S. president on January 20, 1981. Reagan
was a few weeks shy of his seventieth birthday at his first inauguration, making him the oldest elected president.

when he succeeded William McKinley, who had been
assassinated.

FAMILY LIFE

Family can play an important role in a presidential candidate's success. A candidate's wife and children often appear during the presidential campaign, and other family
members may help raise money, campaign, or even serve
on the staff of presidential candidates.

Several presidents had relatives who also rose to the presidency. John Quincy Adams was the son of President John Adams, and President George H.W. Bush's son, George W. Bush, also was elected president. James Madison and Zachary Taylor were second cousins, and William Henry Harrison was the grandfather of Benjamin Harrison. Fifth cousins Theodore Roosevelt and Franklin Roosevelt both became president.

Most presidents have been married, although not all were married at the time of their election. James Buchanan is the only president who never married. Grover Cleveland, John Tyler, and Woodrow Wilson all married during their presidencies. Tyler and Wilson were remarrying after the deaths of their first wives.

Most presidents have had children, either their own or stepchildren and adopted children. Tyler holds the honor of having the most children: 15. Most presidential children have been adults or at least young adults by the time their fathers became president. The only child of a president ever born at the White House was a daughter of Grover Cleveland.

Most presidents were born in eastern states, with a slight majority from the north. Virginia has produced the most presidents, with eight (Washington, Jefferson, Madison, Monroe, William Henry Harrison, Tyler, Taylor, and Wilson).

PRESIDENT OF THE UNITED STATES

The presidency was the creation of a group of delegates, meeting in a sweltering room in Philadelphia. Their vision, their arguments and debates, shaped an office that

This 1805 oil painting of Thomas Jefferson is by Gilbert Stuart. Jefferson once called the presidency "a splendid misery." The splendor must outweigh the misery: Every four years, prominent people clamor to run for the highest office in the United States.

has produced great leaders, as well as men whose accomplishments are little remembered.

The presidency is much more than simply a reflection of whoever occupies the Oval Office at a particular time in history. Each president brings something unique to the job, but the success or failure of a presidency is shaped by events inside and outside the United States, by events inside and outside the White House. Experienced and skillful Cabinet officers and staff members can strengthen a weak presidency; corrupt or divisive advisors can destroy an otherwise successful presidency.

Thomas Jefferson once described the presidency as "a splendid misery," and Adams wrote, when he succeeded Washington as president, that Washington seemed to be the only one who looked relaxed and happy at the inauguration: "Me thought I heard him think, 'Ay! I am fairly out and you are fairly in! See which of us will be the happiest!'"

Nonetheless, the presidency remains a potent symbol of what is unique about the American system of government. Every four years, the American people have an opportunity to choose the person they feel is best qualified to lead the country, and to earn a place in history.

GLOSSARY

ambassador The highest-ranking diplomatic representative appointed by one country to represent it in another country.

bill A draft of a law before it is enacted by a legislature.

cabinet A body of official advisors to a president; in the United States, it consists of the heads of various government departments.

campaign A race between candidates for political office.

caucus A meeting of a group of people belonging to the same political party or faction, usually to select candidates, elect convention delegates, or decide on policy.

constitution A document that sets down the fundamental laws and principles of a government.

consul A person appointed by a government to serve its citizens and business interests in a foreign city.

Electoral College An assembly elected by the voters to perform the formal duty of electing the president and vice president of the United States; the electors of each state are expected to cast their votes for the candidates chosen by popular vote in their state.

impeach To bring a public official before the proper tribunal on charges of wrongdoing.

inauguration The formal ceremony inducting a public official into office.

Joint Chiefs of Staff A group within the Department of Defense consisting of the chief of staff of the Army, the chief of naval operations, the chief of staff of the Air Force, the commandant of the Marine Corps, a director, and a chairman.

pardon The release of a person from further punishment for a crime.

patronage The power to make appointments to government jobs, especially for political advantage.

policy A principle, plan, or course of action pursued by a government, organization, or individual.

primary election An election of voters of a given political party to nominate candidates for public office.

State of the Union The annual event in which the president reports on the status of the country, normally before a joint session of Congress.

treaty A formal agreement between two or more countries, relating to peace, alliances, trade, or other issues.

veto The power of the president to refuse to sign a bill passed by Congress; the bill is prevented from becoming law unless it is passed again with a two-thirds majority by both houses of Congress.

BIBLIOGRAPHY

American Enterprise Institute. *A Discussion With Gerald R. Ford: The American Presidency*. Washington, D.C.: The American Enterprise Institute for Public Policy Research, 1977.

Burke, John P. *Becoming President*. Boulder, Colo.: Lynne Rienner Publishers, 2004.

Colman, Edna M. *Seventy-five Years of White House Gossip: From Washington to Lincoln*. Garden City, N.Y.: Doubleday, Page & Co., 1925.

Congressional Quarterly. *Cabinets and Counselors: The President and the Executive Branch*. Washington, D.C.: Congressional Quarterly Inc., 1989.

Congressional Quarterly. *Powers of the Presidency*. Washington, D.C.: Congressional Quarterly Inc., 1989.

Cunliffe, Marcus. *The American Heritage History of the Presidency*. New York: American Heritage Publishing Co., 1968.

Ellis, Joseph J. *His Excellency: George Washington*. New York: Alfred A. Knopf, 2004.

Koenig, Louis W. *The Chief Executive*, 3rd ed. New York: Harcourt Brace Jovanovich, 1975.

Nelson, Michael (ed.). *Historic Documents on the Presidency, 1776–1989*. Washington, D.C.: Congressional Quarterly Inc., 1989.

Pfiffner, James P. *The Strategic Presidency*, 2nd ed. Lawrence, Kan.: University Press of Kansas, 1996.

Thomas, Norman C., Joseph A. Pika and Richard A. Watson. *The Politics of the Presidency*. Washington, D.C.: Congressional Quarterly Inc., 1993.

Web sites

American Presidents: Life Portraits
www.americanpresidents.org

Center for American Women and Politics
www.cawp.rutgers.edu

Cornell Law School: United States Constitution
www.law.cornell.edu/constitution/

Federal Election Commission
www.fec.gov

History News Network
www.historynewsnetwork.com

Kids Voting U.S.A.
www.kidsvotingusa.org

The Library of Congress: American Memory
www.memory.loc.gov/ammem/

National Geographic
www.nationalgeographic.com

National Park Service: History and Culture
www.cr.nps.gov

100 Milestone Documents
www.ourdocuments.gov

Smart Voter
www.smartvoter.org

U.S. News Classroom
www.usnewsclassroom.com

The White House
www.whitehouse.gov

The White House Historical Association
www.whitehousehistory.org

FURTHER READING

Bausum, Ann. *Our Country's Presidents*. New York: National Geographic Children's Books, 2005.

Grace, Catherine O'Neill. *The White House: An Illustrated History*. New York: Scholastic, 2003.

Rubel, David. *Scholastic Encyclopedia of the Presidents and Their Times*. New York: Scholastic, 2005.

St. George, Judith. *So You Want to Be President?* New York: Philomel Books, 2000.

Travis, Cathy. *Constitution Translated for Kids*. Austin, Texas: Synergy Books, 2006.

Web sites

American President
www.americanpresident.org

Ben's Guide to U.S. Government for Kids
http://bensguide.gpo.gov

Commission on Presidential Debates
www.debates.org

The Democracy Project
www.pbskids.org/democracy/

Ease History
www.easehistory.org

Presidential Museums
www.presidentialmuseums.com

The White House
www.whitehouse.gov

PICTURE CREDITS

INDEX

ABOUT THE AUTHOR

Heather Lehr Wagner is a writer and editor. She is the author of more than 30 books exploring social and political issues and focusing on the lives of prominent men and women. She earned a B.A. in political science from Duke University and an M.A. in government from the College of William and Mary. She lives with her husband and family in Pennsylvania.